CW00404327

RED HANDED

JLM Morton is a writer and poet based in Gloucestershire, England. Winner of the Laurie Lee and Geoffrey Dearmer prizes, her poems appear in *The Poetry Review, The Rialto, Magma, Living With Water* (MUP, 2023), and elsewhere. Morton's work explores rural experience and belonging, ancestry, place and practices of care, repair and solidarity across human and other-than-human worlds. *Red Handed* is her first poetry collection.

Red Handed

JLM Morton

Broken Sleep Books

ISBN: 978-1-916938-20-5

Cover designed by Aaron Kent

Edited by Charley Barnes

Typeset by Aaron Kent

Broken Sleep Books
PO Box 102
Llandysul
SA44 9BG

CONTENTS

I

II

III

I

AN INHERITANCE OF WATER

When I die the chemical signature in my bones
will tell of Thames and Severn, Churn and Frome,

marrow of upland pastures, mill race and outflow.
An ancestral line of dockers loading and unloading cargo.

A spring-fed apple tree that transpires deep in a valley
sheds fruit that only wasps will feed on.

And I want to close my ears to the endless sound
of buckets emptying and refilling on the wheel.

Is this what we call beauty? Is this
a place my hands can hold, still reaching for the world?

None of this is clean but it connects. Big enough
and continuous to contain all of our lives, our deaths

are carried in my blood and breath is carried by water.
Rain is another name for love.

HALF-TIMBERED BOX

I crack off the lid
with a crowbar
and air rushes out
like rain-spoiled wheat
from a chute, one sheep bolts out,
then another and another with a
muffled voice far-away, *yan
tan,* cramming the hallway with fleece
and bleating and the box voice
is counting *yan tan tethera,* I peer
inside, find a model village and a dale
growing there, thistled and ruminant,
raw wool baled and stacked
at the stone cottage doors, *methera pip*
getting louder, I lean over to grab
the lid but a tree comes hurtling
upwards, *methera pip azar,* crashing
through my ceiling, the boughs are strung
with skeins of white-haired folk, bony
fingers beckoning me over the hiss and click
of their knitting machines - they want me
to know where I'm from, so I climb, hoisting
myself past great granddad Thomas
and his *yanadik tanadik* twelve siblings
working the frames with nothing but
rags, swinging my legs from
John to Mercy, Timothy to Sarah, Samuel
to some shit hole near Leeds Bradford Airport

and the passing gust of an airbus — whoosh — and
I walk into a sheepskin hanging
from a branch, air's thin, can't breathe, I'm shivering
and a bearded man in a bottle green cape shouts
over the jets, nods with arms outstretched, *sezer
akka!* throws me a broadcloth, *yannadik tannadik,*
and I catch it, pull it on, unsteady
as a newborn lamb.

LEANING INTO THE TROUBLE

Would you believe
me if I told you

that I walked out
one night

to the Common
and my hands began

to bleed — not blood,
but dye — and the moon

rose on the Scots pine singing
broken hearted in Van Diemen's Land.

With each cold step
there was a tearing as if

time were being torn
like cloth from a frame

and the sea came crashing
over, warm waves

of bioluminescence
carrying iron chains

and the yoke's
dull clunk. I fell

to my knees, scraped
the soil, turned up gold

with my fingers and the moon
cried an ocean for *lutruwita,*

for the riches and the thieving,
and my pilfering hands kept

streaming red and I don't
think they put this

in the history books.

NO ONE WANTS TO TALK ABOUT THE FACTS

Boil 3lbs alum, 6lbs argol and 4pts tin liquor in a vat for thirty minutes.

Trade arms with Native Americans for beetles
swept from the pads of prickly pears to obtain 1lb cochineal.

Sow madder seeds, tend, grow for two years,
then pull up roots at least one half-man long to get 3lbs.

Add both and boil for ten minutes.

Add 60lbs woollen military cloth
spun from Cotswold fleece raised on milkwort and white clover.

Boil for two hours.

Drain cloth.

Collect tins of piss from weavers' dwellings.
Scrape cudbear from the limbs of birch and ash and oak.

Immerse for two hours.

Stretch cloth on tenterhooks to dry on racking fields at Rodborough.

Brush with teasels.

Roll to produce a sheen so bright it turns the nation's heads.

BRUSH THIS UNDER THE CARPET

Shears snip at a coastline, tearing it back
like fleece from a sheep.

Graded, sorted, scoured and drawn
on the warp and weft of the globe.

THE STOREHOUSE OF EARTHLY DATA GOES DEEPER
THAN HUMAN RECORDS

As if becoming broad cloth
I lay myself out flat

chin resting on knuckles
to read   up close   the mee maw

of grass, sheep, wool, water.

I want to disappear
          become a husk.

Windblown and weightless

words become seeds, scattered
in the dips and folds of mother
tongue.

      Feral
          as the teasel grows,

scratching at the nap
of the old tales.
          Tearing the threads.

HOW A SIKSIKÁ HEADDRESS ENDS UP IN AN ENGLISH MUSEUM

The hands I don't know. The hands this trail of cloth passed through, like a red bride. From shepherd to shearer to spinner to weaver to dyer to fuller to shearsman. To boatman adventurer, who bartered the cloth on the Hudson Bay.

To fur trader.

To Siksiká

> who used a needle to sew the length of red cloth
> to the headband.

Did it slip and prick your finger as you threaded through the weave
— did you drop some blood on the red?

How can I know the name of your first love? Was your favourite bird a cardinal or a snow goose; a hawk or a blue jay?

These things are not just objects.

The smell of gunfire carries over grassland. How far was fear triggered by that first repeating rifle?

Let me begin with the cost of the fertiliser made from your own buffalo's bones.

Let me begin with something I don't know.

FALLING GLADLY OFF THE WAGON THAT ROLLED SO SILENTLY

Last Thursday my thirst bettered me
and I drank the Stroudwater Canal

all eight miles of it down in one
long swallow. I can't stop barking

like the paddleboarder's spaniel,
picking at the tail hair in my teeth.

Once I'd got over the mute swan's egg,
the trolley and milk-bottled mud,

I choked on brick at Nutshell Bridge.
Tasted coal, lung tonic, the dust

of widow-makers settled in
the gunwale of a Severn Trow.

Bow-hauled by ghosts, I got high
on tea and opium, madder than a stroud.

My guts foundered on tradecloth,
the theft of New World skin and bone —

all my depth perception's gone,
I've let the flock go to my head.

This is how I'm craving
with sickness for the dead.

WING DUST LEAVES ITS REMNANTS UPON ME

Moth wants the light,
        which is the wool.
Eats it in hectares,
teaching its lesson about clothes.

Mutualities and dependencies,
biomass and extinction,
moths and their holes.

Moth will eat hats, dolls and toys;
my cashmere gloves, my Afghan shawl —
the holes are (a) shame.

(I didn't know I was a moth. I thought
I was just the pulled threads
of the hole. A shoddy casement.)

What of mending and repair?
The arrogance of not darning.

Can the hole say something or
nothing at all?

We come into the world through holes,
such is the hole's paradox,
the moth's cocoon.

These days, the world seems made
of people who are moths
and those who are holes.

The world reproduces itself
through a small aperture
in a darkened room.

All that wanting fluttering over the walls.

TOWN HAS NO HISTORY EXCEPT IT BE THAT OF THE RISE AND PEACEFUL PROGRESS OF THE WOOLLEN CLOTH TRADE

Limestone is an animal, a bunch of shells and skeletons, raised up from a crowded sea. I mean Archway is a national fact, as in mild and kindly countryside, as in 1834, the year the memorial arch was built. Gateway to a mansion and the only British monument to abolition. Oh irony, but not.

By this I mean there was a time when I didn't know that cashew nuts grow on fruit looking like a hybrid of pepper and squash. File that under *this seems like a hoax, but isn't*, how that fruit fell apart in my hands and stained my shirt yellow as we sped from Kano to Jos in a cab called Freedom and I had it all. As in freedom. I ate it all up.

The archway still stands, tucked away in a corner of a T-junction, the sweep of the drive long gone, as in a memory of confidence now flanked by council houses, a whole new kind of estate. As in right to buy. I mean isn't the past a lesson, not a life sentence.

The perception of being in a long tunnel, bright lights, as in all people, everyone, equal in death. A sense of benign detachment. I mean when I was ten I found out that one day I will die. I crouched behind the sofa in my volcanic body watching the Indians get killed by cowboys — hundreds of them shot with bullets. Except an overwhelming feeling of peaceful.

Archway as in it's complicated. Meaning at the Wesleyan chapel on Acre Street complaints were made about the women getting up petitions. As in suffrage, as in emancipation, as in another great national invention, as in keep quiet about the hunger strikes, force feeding, decency and the King's horse.

Archway as in particular, as in unique in character, as in eccentric. To be removed from the centre, as in exceptional, team games, home ownership, Ordnance Survey, hypocrisy, the royal household, gardening, being quirkily brave, precision as in a lightning bolt that's 30,000 degrees centigrade, or five times hotter than the surface of the sun. My best t-shirt when I was ten had a lightning flash on it and my mum said *lightning never strikes twice*, as in, made me feel special.

Chiaroscuro, meaning the often-dramatic contrast between light and shade in art, is one of the most mispronounced words in, as in stumbled over, as in stammered through, the English language. As in shame gains power from being unspeakable. I mean radical shadow, light as a refusal of shade, as in we contain irreconcilable multitudes, as in satire, consolation, back-lash. Except in 1834, God only freed the children who were under six years old. As in a proud British boast, except History is how we choose the past. I mean time is created by things; it isn't just there waiting for those things to act inside it. As in time is relative, moving more slowly if an object is moving fast, like a taxicab or a rock-hard ball of fossilised shells thrown through a window.

HAND ME DOWN

So much depends
upon

a fierce vindictive scribble
of red.

Ships of foam, the stained
stones

kissed by the English
dead.

THE SQUEAKING HINGE ON THE PUB SIGN HAS BEEN TRYING TO SAY LOOK

how they haunt
    this hinge of high land.

Blue Boys
    linger

between common ground
    and the new estate.

Look to the night sky
    an *indigo bonanza*

emptied into their vat.
    But first, the ocean

its currency of brass manillas
    and lines of chained men.

Somewhere a white girl is plunged
    in her vegetable world

commanding the plants
    to set root.

Black girls are
    raised for blue dye

pounding the leaves
    to break. Ferment.

Strain and sun-dry.
    The stench.

Each bale is bloodied
      and bound,

carried on the sea's
      rough hands

to the Blue
      Boys who pass on

their art with colour that only
      comes true on the air.

COLOUR IS A CANARY SPECIES FOR ENLIGHTENMENT

Weld in a boiling vat makes a fine yellow,
plucked yellowhammer feather kind of yellow.

Waste ground hugging, random flowering
behaviour, tall, curved spires of yellow.

Sloshing mordant piss from a shoulder yoke,
stumbling step turns chalk to yellow.

A yolk breaks on the Severn, sunlight scatters
teasel seeds, the fuller's earth hue yellow.

Stowed with pepper, dyewood, ivory,
a brig is quarantined, a jack flag yellow.

Look up. I will do the same and think of you
my love, the North Star blazing yellow.

Could I be the flame that licked the chimney -
East India Company opium yellow?

Tea, gazebos, flock wallpaper — the moment
all the cash gets blown on Speculation is yellow.

I am a dog riot running hares to ground,
the line from Square to Castle, Berkeley yellow.

Am I too loud for you? Too incandescent?
I rebound off your eyes, is it? Tennis yellow.

There is no name for the sound of the circling buzzard —
but if there were it would be yellow.

Indigo Bonanza!

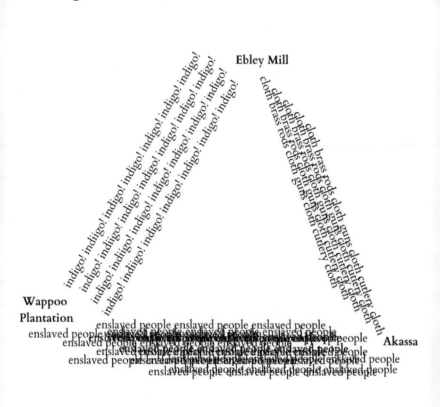

BODIES REMEMBER SUCH HISTORIES, EVEN WHEN WE FORGET THEM

I am spreadeagled taut
on the paddles of a waterwheel.

I try to convert,
to save myself

with the energy of water
the running dyes

the green the yellow
the red the blue on the rollers.

Everything that turns is a mill.

My bones are fused to the loom, my skin
is raised and shorn to a perfect finish.

A dirty habit stretched on tenterhooks.

Every mill has turned me out.

If anyone wants to know
my future, I would gentle
the foundations of fleece and brook.

Tender the generosity of the pond.

If I were to ask you to guess the world's most wanted colour —

Not a chest of it reached England without the stain of human.

Darkened as if by bruising,

In the womb of the vat there is life.

Gnosis at temporal frequency in the third eye.

Oxygen turned sorcerer, colour of the devil's dye.

SELF-SELF CONSIDERS HISTORICAL SELF; OR, WHY TALK ABOUT THESE PEOPLE WHEN WE CAN SHY AWAY

from the danger
but I want
to know
██████████ of
Eliza ████ ████████.

██████████ woman.
inventor.
██████████.

George Washington a pall
bearer at her funeral.

First important.
Mere girl.

████.

████.

Indigo farmer.

████.

She haunts me.

I haunt her back.

Like any good daughter.

TURNING IT AROUND AND AROUND AND AROUND

How do you hold the past?

      As a tender leaf
    translucent in sun light,

or the green hope of thread
    rising from dye pits?

Perhaps as a rock of blue gold.

LETTERS AND MEMORANDA FROM A SIXTEEN-YEAR-OLD WHITE GIRL

I flatter myself   my lott has fallen here
much friendship Civility   polite, agreeable
very much in the English taste.

The Country is in General fertile and abounds.
Imployed in business   the business of three plantations
much writing   more business   much business.

Greater hopes from the Indigo   in preference.
The loss of a   man, the pleasure of a line from you —
so great a blessing.   A barrel of butter.

LIFECYCLE OF THE COCHINEAL BEETLE, c.1788

An egg breaks on the pad of a prickly pear somewhere
in Oaxaca where the scale insects' livid bodies

mass and crackle in the sun. Emerging, a crawler nymph
clusters with the softness of her siblings

to feed in the downy blanket – explorers edging
to the brink of the known world.

Nymph throws out a long wisp of wax,
a thread to catch a ride on the wind, lifting and

landing on the terra incognita of a new cactus pad.

Her claim is staked with a stab of her beak.

Cochineal sups the juices, sees off predators
— lacewings, ladybirds, ants — with the bright surprise

of her body. Fat, fierce and full of poison. She
has detached her wings. Has no need of legs.

Holding her colour quietly in trust – she waits
for the male to eat his fill, to mate and die.

Scraped away at ninety days, her body is laid out
and dried, pulverised. Destined for dominion.

SAY MY NAME

... if dung is not enough, he is to find it.
— Strachan & Co. contract, Lodgemore Mill

They are cleverer than you think, the pigs.
Learn a command quicker than dogs, will pigs.

Would you have me sing of some weaver girl?
I wish for blindness, to wallow with pigs.

The flesh of gilts and sows is rose petals.
Daybreak disembowels, eats my heart, pigs.

Someday I'll move to the higher up slopes —
where the orchids grow, you don't feel the pigs.

For what is breath but the movement of air.
One vessel to another, pigs to pigs.

Bleed out a universe on a stone floor,
skin and split, they die piece by piece, the pigs.

Call me Pig Man, call me Joe Say, my name —
see my life ablaze in a stye of pigs.

ON THE SOULS
at Wallbridge Mill, now a vets

The venetian window, which today seems to us
just a dirty light to shed on the animals,
can open itself like a poem, singing quietly

and backwards to summon the ghosts —
over the bins and the portacabin
up to the old yard.

This paned creature stinks of machine oil
and raw wool, carrying comfort
to the unnoticed and the harried

with their ledgers of profit and loss:

-    one suit of flea-ridden shoddy
-    an eye lost to the flying shuttle
-    a loaf of bread pulled from the flames

A reckoning caught in the glass.

CLASS WAR PEP TALK TO FLOCK WALLPAPER

And what? Like a dumb beast,
you wanted to frott your owners
with your fuzzy surfaces.

Show them how grateful.

You have been pasted up, an indulgence
under gilt-framed portraits. You set off
the sugar loaf and the walnut bureau.

Once you were a noble sheep.

Tell them to enter a room of blades. See how
they like being chopped to a powder. Flocked!

Have them pummelled on a sieve, held down
with animal glue. Papered onto the walls.

This isn't what anyone should be calling
home — no care here for the tilting ears
or the tone of a call.

Affection is so non-U.

There but for the grace of —

own the stinking shit that clumped to your back legs
and your flyblown asshole where the maggots thrived.

Is that not also a burnishing?

HOMO 3681, AT THE HUNTERIAN MUSEUM

... a very sensible and ingenious practitioner of physic ... has preserved those five children in spirits; and, if desired, he will send them for the inspection of the Society.

— Letter from Dr Blane to Dr Garthshore, June 22nd, 1786.

A perspex frieze of spirit and wet tissue
now holds their choral mouths,
their quartered skulls, their scalps
like stocking toes: a weaver's pride.

They say you were just twenty-one
when your waters burst five times,
delivering three dead, two living.

The first at two p.m.,
the last at ten to three.
Such symmetry.
All girls.

I wonder did you wonder
at the kick of her with trousered skin,
at the gully where her heart should've been,
at her wings of butterflied bone?

Did you hold your nerve when
your body grew each day,
when your clothing was
unpicked and then resewn?
When drenched in breeding sweats,
did that doctor ask — prevail — for your consent?
Perhaps you didn't care for sentiment.
Perhaps you shouldered grief,

lifted pails of grain with eyes smoothed shut
and walked the two miles home.

Perhaps you didn't hear the last born —
poised, the dancer with loose fists —
when she pressed her tongue tip to her palate
and said *love*

DON'T GIVE ME ANYTHING AS MANGLED AS THIS
FEELING

No word of a lie I found it   laid out on the
mudflats   let off by the tide   I had to have
it   redcoat   stinking reeking hanging to be
honest with crude oil salt and the veld hooked
it up with a finger to sniff it wet wool itching at
my nose shrugged it on anyway redcoat got a
pace on couldn't stop my legs from marching
marching country house trout fishing on
a chalk stream heading home through the
territory of the Vale country lanes and cow
parsley to be fair pride and rough cloth at the
neck holding my head high *get in you rogue!*
back in my lounge I'm not lying the slither
of wool on wool was deafening the crack of
a whip the window opening and the play of
rousing fife and drums drifted over the hill
didyousaymynamewasZachariahnow?   so
rousing a certain breed of English sanity stiff
upper   you understand   hedgerows I kept
shifting considering my position what the fuck
is this anyway? trying to catch it can you hear
that? I asked them neighbours nothing no joy
        an albatross flew overhead
later in Tesco Express I lost it in the redcoat
smashing up the chiller cabinets grabbing off
the shelves   sugar rice fags cocoa rum   and
I won't lie I felt alive *alive!* revolting with

a feeling I could have anything and anyone I
wanted arrestable to be fair   got away with
it I'd say *Frickin' nutcase* was all that cashier
had when they charged me through the
queues slung my body down on the forecourt
I tried to spot wash the blood coat with spit
on a hankie   fully made a proper mess of
mending the seams   went to the dry cleaners
to see if they could fix it but fairplay I knew
what was on her mind from the way she slow
chewed her gum and looked me up and down
say no more

THE KISS

Where the sheep have cracked
a path in the egg of the hill
you will find the mizzle hush
of these dull hibernal days —
the bluster shoves you on
to a place where even the crows'
black prayers take shelter.

Where the path turns on the oval,
a hawthorn bush scrawls
love letters to the wind,
telling how it holds bright keys
of mistletoe in its language
of spikes and membranes.

The corals and dun of lichen
nurtured on the branches
 say
  this
   is
    patience —

come snag
your unready heart.

LOVE SONG FOR EWE

No beast grazes a hill as I do, ruminating
on forbs and clover, the panopticon
of my rectangular pupils set in gold.
Count me, my lover, tup your coins.
For you I would kneel without lameness,
which is to say I'll remember if you go.
I'm on the run with all the lustre
of my fleece, I leap the gate,
make of the dell a fire in my wake.
The turn of a branch has nothing
on your improbable limbs, the pride
in the angles of your skull.
Follow me as I follow you
to each blade of grass.
We will eat in the noiseless altitude.
We will feast on the summit.

LORD CHANCELLOR'S SEAT IS A RED WOOLSACK

I stole
a hand towel
from the cloakroom
in the House
of Lords

white
with
a red stripe

through
the
centre

a cloth
for the butcher
and his slab
of faded
meat.

MEND WITH PEACE, MEND WITH CARE

CAN I LIVE WITH WHAT I HAVE TO SAY

It's unexpected, the watermeadow
below the flyover,

this softness underfoot
beneath the cantilevered concrete,

the deafening of freight's
crass lexicon.

Tired pilgrim, I stumble on
through sodden sedge,

startling roe deer as if
I was the one who didn't belong.

Here is where the sour things grow.
Sloe, crab apple, rowan.

Grand old narratives
of woolsack and red cloth,

derelict groundworks of ridge and sluice.
Water that's always already elsewhere.

I have learned to read
the land's biography,

wishing for a kinder future
than what lies in these ruins.

May the rowing boat laid over
a leat be a crossing place

for the heart's repair,
a blessing of water, earth and air.

May the fire in the poplars make anew.

II

SENTIENT

Blackbird grammar — quick statements pursued to the point of amazement, then silence.
— Alice Oswald

hedge/witch

    on the scarp rim

    rock worn

       frost needled

play
the
line

between

wild_and_world

    be the buzzard
read the palm
    of sky

find grass
    has ceased
       to grow

cloud's thin garland

       hangs

at the grey smudge

of the near horizon

solstice   standstill

sun   stands   still

see
the mountains
again

insistent sandstone
cone of Sugar Loaf

all this survival

                grasping
         last brambles
like the –

  or traveller's joy smothering life

see what hope

this tongue and bone of a season

test a body on a steep
incline
  throat catch
wind strip
  the newborn
        year

fine as hogweed filaments
             trembling
               firmament

put away satin beauty moth
in the yew's hold

percuss the nettle sting

name   perihelion

                earth   moves

                        faster

stop water ___ a solid state

glaze blackened dogrose hips
the old dock patch

see the ash trees fall

                one

                by

                one

                by

                one

                their absence a sky's

grief   the gut

                stun

 of their cut trunks

    this quaking earth
  does not predict

there will be no revelations
   only   un-spool-ings

 a heart
through leaf litter
rude and green

the quiet place
                 of a col
                      lapsed
                       elder

         ivy
         entrails
         clutch
         the
         innermost
         parts
         wild arum
         folk
         tender ear
         poison arrow
         cows and bulls
         wake robin
         sonsie give us your hand
         naming
         stallions and mares
         frog's meat
         cuckoo pint
         adder's root
         priest's pintle
         babe in the cradle
         bobbins
         glut

their pollen will come
  to light
           the wooded
                      way
  burnt brook banks
off the old bottle dump
 tinkling their language
  of glass and crockery

         don't
         cut

first primrose
yellow as an elder's eye
blinking

slide high
on jade milk
river after
thaw

alder haze the bank

reap the gorseflower
     root into
     this foodless
 crucible of carbon

       conjure false spring!

          rain
                          after
rain
                singing   after
          blackbird   singing

first
                     blackbird
  singing

                     after
                          rain

taste the wild
  garlic   bear's onion
               stinking
past
   the cold front
past the rough
   medicine of borage
see off our fevers
   goosegrass the season's
borderlands, not yet sticky
          enough to cleave

touch the
toad   pass
through
the
thin

place
ancestral breeding pond

 blackthorn last in
fruit, first in bloom
  pollen cap the anthers
beckon   bees
  beetles sleep
          sleep on
                  sleep on

three white willows at the spring
branches so ready to
          ignite
          the
          blue
          flame
          of sky

do not say
the early colour
of spring is not green

it is arterial red

how catkins talk
in
trembling
ochre
tongues

III

SECRETS OF MATTER AND SPIRIT

I hold my mother
within me, the way stone
is made up of minerals,
the ossified body of a mollusc,

the memory of heat in quartz.

If I frame the statue's face
with my camera, see
her robust arms draw in,
it is my child asking me
to guard the warm spot as she runs

to another room and returns,
jumping back in just to feel
the weightlessness.

My grandmother is a hare
running at speed, eyes set high
with an orbital range. I am seen.
And the hare's gaze rests upon me.

I rest, the way the weather
has worn soft the statue's ministrations.

This is how I hold the fragment,
as if the weight is something

I could travel through

and the places where
touch has lightened the patina
are pathways to the sacred.

Climb inside my mother's
mother's mother's urn and see

how it is filled with fireflies.

Hounds and children curl
around my legs. What sound
is there for this ritual?

Perhaps a growl, long and steady,

as my camera frames
the face of the *mater*.

Sometimes the rain extinguishes.
But the body is a record,
mongrel strata layered
with different versions of childhood,
barking and simpering
in their Jurassic furs. Yet loyal
as stone.

Which is how
I would like to be held.

WHAT THE WATERCOURSE CARRIES

squinting at the screen

       Brythonic **Cymraeg** Breton Kernewek Cambric

as if to translate

     the source

as if language is a window

or warm air trapped behind

     glass

a tank / a screen / a kitchen

     Avon afon aven avon

 listen –   few inscriptions

Celtic **on a lead tablet** curses the

worthless woman

         no documents

              I have bound

a word / a glint / a scale

may I **speaks** *oh divine*

     water, tears

      *dubri dŵr dour dowr

      Exe

      Axe

      Esk

our home rivers outlast us

      *ēskos Usk

abounding in fish

     and connect

fish eskUskskUs pysg

     fishgodpysgod **pysgod dwyfol**

oh divine **fish-god-dess**

     mouth-mother

        source

          surfacing

FIELD NOTE, CHURCH

I reached back to the past and found invasion, colonisation and magic in the notion that the ice melt of the river we know now precedes human habitation. The name of the River Churn is pre-Roman, thought to have its origins in the ancient Celtic language spoken by the Dobunni who lived here before the first-century conquest. Below Coberley and Coleford, the river runs through Bagendon, the Dobunni's fortified capital and evidence has been found along the river of Romano-Celt ritual and worship in sacred waters, manifested in a local goddess cult. Following deer desire paths along the bank, my ankles tingled from the nettle stings, shoes full of gravel and mud, sunk into the beds of irises below the old poplars not yet in leaf. Pilgrim. Votive.

YOU RUN THROUGH ME

your   whole life   ahead
    behind   around   a whole
   floodplain   of pastness
    and presence   compressed
into   oolite   blue clay   cornbrash
                              urgent
     as longing
            dragging
   at my body   water's memory
          is a home   I stumble
                  into
                  the soft plates
          of my feet are pestled
     on the debris of a tropical sea
    and its upheavals
            Cuda
      cuda's   wold
            Cotteswold
    churning
  ex nihilo your
     bodily secretions   wash
my   body

            is
            here
                  reaching for
     your arterial walls
grown thick with fireweed

for the   stink and bloom
of elderflowers growing
in your easy crevices

I clamber on   love
your   winter wreckage
  a wildfire   looking for
the comfort of water
  in the valley of nettles
dead trees snagged
  with feedbags
grey-green sludge
  amphibious tails
          of filth

I am full   with   the smell
    of water mint
          with   longing with
  grabbing   over   wire stock fence
    I bring bread and apples
  to your stone relief
    spilling my blood
  on your mineral bones

like a fool   holding fast
  to a notion of permanence

  I reach for you

you run through me

precaution against grief

you're there

are you there

are you there

WE BECOME WITH EACH OTHER OR NOT AT ALL

They stunned me with the force
of a shifting age. Like asteroids,
farming, the internet. Mother goddesses,
a sacred three in the hot displays
at the Roman Baths. To my shame, I gasped.
I almost cried, while tourists hustled
for selfies with the Gorgon's Head
and the Façade of the Four Seasons. I was
roped to the spot by an invisible line to

the votive relief in the glass. Carved
grey schist - hard yet brittle - the workings
of the sculptor still visible and Celtic, here
before the Romans. Three mother goddesses
with naked breasts, their pleated skirts, the tilt
of movement in their smooth round heads.
Linked together arm in arm — more sisters
than mothers.

Driving home I caught sight of the familiar
line at a high point on the horizon —
beech trees planted in perfect definition
with the light behind them. The escarpment
from an era when mountains formed
and the forests became coal and carboniferous
rock — or schist. How like the rings of trees
were the heads of the mother goddesses.

How like the curvature of the earth.
The gravity of our home place holding us here.
They and I at different ends of this vanishing
human season.

RITUAL FOR SAFE PASSAGE THROUGH CHILDBIRTH

before dawn
the expectant mothers creep

from their houses in the suburbs
where water still seeps up
        t
        a
        r
        m
        a
through the c

trickles of it, glistening
in the dark

they drop their votive p
            i
            n
            s
through the cracks at the kerbside
hear them drop — *ting*!

onto millions, the millions heaped
before them, into the springs

IF FEAR COULD BE DEFLESHED

Every walk is a plea

a prayer on the song flight
of the skylark.

An appeal

for the day and its tasks,
for the world and its needs.

I climb

to The Toots tomb shrine,
looking for communion
with the dead.

My feet are cut on shards
at the bottle dump, the tiny pottery
of infection surfaces
in my warrened wounds.

And each day from the chamber
of my tired mind
a different soul answers.

Today - my grandmother,
clean and ritual,
clatters her undone bones.

And the wind mutters her incantations,
teaching what mothers teach -

that the tides of the estuary are tireless,
that the mate of the magpie is always near.

I feel the cloud's ontology,
the certainty of shadow on land

pushing me from the mound
and on my way, teaching love

and survival.
Sometimes with sorrow.

DEVOTIONAL

I think the stones say
Dear bastard.

Walking on the frozen hill
I read messages
in objects.

The spilled petals
spell out *d-a-r-l-i-n-g h-u-m-a-n.*
An empty bottle

of cheap Corbières signs
the delicious musk of morning sex.

Is the true gift
of our devotion
what saves us

from the gut trench
of a crow's call,

from frost-burnt stems,
the dew and spit in the dregs?

These votives are the alphabet
of an ancient hand,

scrawled on the brute remembrance
of our high places.

Every syllable a question that asks
if prayers still have any meaning.

WE SWALLOW OUR ANCESTORS AND ALL THAT HAS GONE BEFORE

A pair of broken glasses from above,
ghosts on the worked field.
One rimmed lens and another conjoined.

To the north, two thick lines,
a dark dot where the entrance
must have been.

Bones long ploughed into the earth —
monuments to ancient lives
and this is all we have.

Levelled remains transferred
so entirely to the soil
that grows the food we eat.

The traces of our lives,
the marks that we have made.
The proof that we were here.

TO THE CROWD CONTROL BARRIER

blocking the footpath to the lake
I say what is your provenance

can the pig iron and the ores
in the nursery of your bones
age the carp by the thickness of its scales

can your chain of custody hold
spike rush, speedwell, fleabane, bedstraw
in the un-historied lines of your cage

you cannot certify the emeralds
of the beautiful demoiselle
threading desire through the reedbeds

this place cannot be detained
from soothing the torrents,
weighing each tusk, each tooth,

each mammoth rounding things out
with the flow of Churn, Coln, Leach
and an abdominal love

teaching me pity
for the conceit of your claim
on this house of water.

WINGSPAN

Have you seen the white magpie, have you
watched it pick through the grass
at water's edge, its head a pumpjack
drawing up invertebrate treasure,
a one in a million portent
of your own *untapped potential*.

What if the sight of it could change your life,
make you more than passing traffic,
more than a litter bin scavenge
for sandwich crusts in a clingfilm tangle,
more than a strutting spar with a
loose flock of associates.

Would you unfold your wings in the branches
of the soft leaved birch, enter the water
and feel it not as a foe to be challenged,
but as a friend to be met.
Accept that the dare of being here
is all the luck you need.

On the far side of a copse of beech and hazel saplings, there was a narrow wooden bridge crossing the River Churn where the water was high summer singing as it flowed low over the stones. The last time I had been here was as a small child to watch the fireworks, but I hardly knew it, this hinterland on the other side of town from the one I grew up on. I was following the river from City Bank nature reserve along the back of Purley Road in Cirencester. In places the water was crowded out by plant life — overhanging willow, gunnera, rosebay willowherb and brambles in flower — abundant, vibrant matter.

The crows were coming noisily into roost on this soft golden evening as I emerged from the bridge and the trees onto an open field where the river runs along the margin. Three boys in hooded tops were playing ball and chatting happily on the other side of the field. We didn't speak but I could feel the curious gaze of these benevolent godlets on me as I looked for a gap in the bank to get down into the water. I got in up to my ankles and trod carefully along the riverbed, trying not to disturb the rocks that gave shelter to fish and invertebrates. A trio of dragonflies skipped on the air around me.

I ducked down to walk through an arched red brick tunnel. The water reflected the last of the sunlight onto the roof and walls that were crumbling and softened with a coating of green algae and moss. It smelt faintly of earthy chalk.

Beyond the bridge the river was clean and prettier than I'd expected, the pale red roots of the overhanging trees fingering the surface of the water from below. A discarded hooded coat waved in the gentle flow, snagged on a fallen branch.

SELF PORTRAIT AS A GUARDIAN SPIRIT

It falls like a language
newly learned, drifts
of words held in a breath
of shale around my shoulders.

Smell of salt and sea fish,
grainy to touch
in the blazing dawn.

This cloak is a god, a spirit
that holds and lets go,
that cowls me from the clean face
of fact.

All this chronology.

The child, the adult, the elder,
the river that will heal, purge
and console.

Stone poultice, fossil guard.

A new stone skin for my soft
impermanence.

A piece of me falls
forward, a piece of me falls
back. Thus the expanding universe.

A scuttling spirit who has travelled
here and found the future.

In rock.
Water.

Something older
than light.

SOMETHING MUTABLE OF PLACE

Genio Sancto Hvivs Loci
— Altar inscription, Corinium

I couldn't find it in the broken statue
or the stillness of the alcove. It cast
uneven pools of light on to my skin
and I chased it, felt it slip around
away from me like shoaling roach.

The sour milk of dandelions
on my tongue. Ancient goat horns
spilt all over
me, a double cornucopia of high wolds,
black foals feeding at dawn, pylons, ploughed fields.

I   stumbled
      in
to   the nettles.

Allowed the river's silt to soothe me.
The darkness of the icehouse.

All of my love became caught
on the filaments in a brachiopod's shell
and my heart took root. A fleshy pedicule
on a hill that was once a shallow sea.

I laid down on a grassy patera,
asked no questions at the altar, cannot say
what it is that I have found, or how.

STONE CALLS US TO THE JOY OF THIS WORLD

squabbling over directions we pull up / to the burial ground and
find the stone interred in leaves / my father the winter bulb /
hollowed of his green fuse /

I store him in the organ of my memory / each day laying rosemary
for remembrance in the hollows / I clear and cleanse the stone /
with the rites of an old sponge that illuminates the carvings /

water glimmering / for *a kind and gentle man*

the wind gets up and urges us / to scatter our mourning / on
the gnarled steep and blackthorn / to the spirit door of the long
barrow where we take shelter / caught out by a sudden change in
weather /

in the stone chamber of the mound / it is not dark at all / there
is the fire of our family burning / gathered round / *indigenes*
carrying our future on a river in spate / our Styx of genetic
instructions / eddying against the storm / and the old land

awakens in us / as we run to circle the barrow three times round /
and laugh all the way back down / without

epiphany / heading west heading home / we're so happy in the
wind and sleet slapping our faces / with its fierce and watchful ice

PORTRAIT OF ROSMERTA AS A LITANY OF COMPLAINTS

Being goddess of prosperity deranged me, all that rotting
flesh left at my feet, the rancid fat I churned

for millennia. Blue bottles stalked me with their revolting metallic,
their faceted eyes, storming my coordinates to throw up.

These stone feet cannot outpace the glut! Supplicants push
on with their pleas, their "need" for bifold doors and bubble butts —

competing for potential. My arms have collapsed with the gifts.
Snakes curl around my staff and open their mouths wide

in ways that turn them into vulva and phallus, divine balance
of caduceus. More re-enchantment. More groundwater rising.

Consort Mercury and I keep the quicksilver truth of a mirror held
all around us — this is the incantation. Love is not battle or surrender.

The statue is not the woman, it is not his body the statue
is a false icon. A history of how we have given.

I unfolded the tissue paper protecting the sketchbooks that show a talented artist working in pencil and watercolour. The smell of lead and old, dry paper drifted up as I turned the pages and recognised many of the places Helen Cripps had drawn. It felt uncanny, close to a feeling of nostalgia, a return to home, a bittersweet yearning. Helen Cripps' sketches were mostly of buildings. I pictured her in the gardens of these houses, painting and sketching while her husband saw to business inside — or perhaps she travelled alone. One was of the view from her bedroom window on The Mead, just at the end of Coxwell Street, looking out towards the church clock tower. It was almost exactly the same view as I'd had from my own bedroom window as a child, just at a slightly different angle, drawing me closer to Helen.

Tucked away at the back of one book were the only sketches of people - the beginnings of a very simple pencil line drawing of a man's face and another of a woman turning away, as if to leave a room. Was this her husband, Wilfred Cripps, and perhaps a self-portrait?

Helen survived Wilfred by more than 30 years, loyally keeping up his interest in church plate and archaeology. From 1918, when women of property over 30 were permitted to vote, Helen appears on the electoral roll every subsequent year until her death.

She was party to the discovery in April 1899 of the three mother goddesses' votive relief (also known as Deae Matres or Sulevaie) found in Ashcroft, almost perfectly preserved. Looking at the dates of her sketches, I realised she and I were the exact same age at the point we both began to discover and explore the mother goddesses. I wonder what they meant to her, if anything, beyond an interesting archaeological find.

As I looked out of the window on the top floor of the Museum among the archives on that March morning, I saw again the same view of the church clock tower over the rooftops drawn by Helen and gazed at for hours by me from my bedroom window as a child. The church, a sacred site for centuries - Roman before Christian, Celtic before Roman — is a place of sanctuary and reflection. I was in a thin place, as if the veil of time and circumstance between myself, Helen and the goddesses was lifting and falling in a gentle breeze.

I WADE THE RIVER SEARCHING FOR HOME

Very clear   pale
holding baskets of bread and fruit
three mother goddesses
summon divinity from stone

very smooth and well-made and cool to the touch
three women   in a thin place
carved in the divinity of stone

certain   calm
three mother goddesses
sense the wounds of a place
summon the power of limestone

the splash of an offering in a shallow spring

a woman in a place
like home   wades in a river
the riverbed gently knuckles her feet
she doesn't know she's looking

for the splash of an offering

a pencil line drawing   very precise   clear
of a woman in a long dress turning
as if to leave a room
an offering

goes to paint
layering pure feeling   wet on dry

the sound   clear and certain
of a bell ringing on the quarter hour
over rooftops   the gold hand
on a black clockface   clicks

she goes to paint
layering pure feeling   wet on dry
a trickling spring
the splash of an offering

a trickling spring
the splash of an offering

a girl, a teen   very alone
looks to the night   from a bedroom window
hears a bell over rooftops
wishes her mother more than stone

the click of heeled boots on the floorboards

looking from a bedroom window over rooftops
a woman struggles
to find divinity in stone

quiet clicking boots of a woman
coming to rest at an easel
she paints   clear   precise

lines of the church tower
her mind scumbles the trees

wading splashing   home on the river
her body an offering to limestone
a woman ducks below overhanging
trees   quiet voices sing far away

a stir   a sense   of a sacred site
when she came for the certainty of stone
her eyes close

very smooth and well-made and cool to the touch
three women in a place
hoping   summoning   divinity from stone

careful   spadework   scraping round
the Roman temple dig
clear   precise   lines marked out
her brush   sweeps the earth aside

discovers three mothers carved in stone
a votive relief   perfectly preserved

timeless

a woman looks through a glass cabinet
at statues and altars   in the Sulevaie
she finds the divinity of home

very composed
a woman's hand smooths the cartridge paper
begins to draw   pencil sound conjures
three figures from lead

an exact scale
a perfect   likeness   the hair swept up on their heads
eyes closed   lips straight
better to receive their requests

so they say   people say
the mothers are death and peace and healing
a sacred three

the one who was
the one who is
the one who is yet to be

surrounded by sketchbooks and statues and archives
a woman looks from a museum window
over familiar rooftops

from the church clocktower   a bell sounds
   clear   precise
   marking out the hours

Sul

Sol

Solstice

Sulevae

Sulis

Sulis Minerva

FURIOUS MAGIC
at the thermal springs, Bath, England.

Below street level in the thermae, sulphur
seeps into the shops and houses

above, evaporates
like a dream of being warm and fed.

Or the hot spring of eight-thousand-year-old rain forced
through a fault.

Not the oracle,
but the premonition itself.

Sulis Minerva. Sun and wisdom.
Solar power. Accept my curses.

Your gut gazers read the portents
of the Earth's bowels sloshing with wine —

keepers of memory, diviners of the future, I beg them
to tell against expectation.

People here still throw their coins in the frigidarium.
I throw mine and wish with all the currency of the world

for defacement by the minerals and the mettle to act
without flinch or falter.

Give me the weather I need. All that drizzle between drought
and flood is the name I keep for your consolations.

Life flickers.

Translucent as the Thin Leaved Whitebeam
or the eye socket of a pale corvid, sacred

conduit between living and dead. All of us
animals among animals –

we are a fixed red thread of common. Each
rotation, every root, could be a revelation,

a tree growing
from this dark powdered cone of green.

CURSE TABLETS

takedowns from the British Celt (an imagined translation)

Everyone who ever loved you
was wrong.

May your mind be
an utter bungalow.

May you go the many miles
you need to reach
unexceptional.

You are
the human equivalent
of a participation award.

May your day be
as scintillating
as your personality.

I envy everyone
you have
never met.

May you
develop
an obsessive compulsion for clean hands.

You are a
breathing
pork pie.

FIELD GUIDE TO THE COTSWOLD HARE

Used to being a deity, these days
Hare feeds on black gold,
oil seeping from their orifices
dripping from tear ducts, nostrils, anus.
Hare's long, black-tipped ears
stream money when they run,
petrol head topping speeds
of forty-five miles an hour,
flurries of bank notes over high
ploughed fields in winter.
Hare's habitat is woodland
where the money grows on trees
and they strip the bark for coin.
Or farmland, where coal has replaced the crops —
Hare leaves sooty tracks wherever they go,
but the predators are all dead now anyway.
It's just the last of the humans to kill.
Hare is known to take a break from spraying
cash all over the countryside and boxing suitors
with bullion clutched in their paws.
Hare can be found resting in *forms* —
shallow depressions in the ground
of private property, lined with crypto and the shame of the penniless,
from which vantage Hare fires oil canons
at migrants lured by permissive paths. These days
(as we know) the rivers are dry and the seasons have
gone, so the wanderers can be easy to mark,
driven by thirst and hunger.

Hare's droppings are sweet smelling, like a damp
bundle of fifty-pound notes with a hint
of natural gas. Though lately it's been said
Hare's bones were barely worth gnawing.

EMBRACE THE BASE
   at the Moderna Museet, Stockholm

The man in the bar tells me Chat GPT is *catastrophic*, *worse
than climate, worse than war. You must use it to write a poem.*

The women's voices call me back with their loose-breasted
flickering figures dragged away at the armpits, singing

from the footage on the screen at the centre of the Monica Sjöö
retrospective.

Carry Greenham home, yes. Cobalt blue, orange, white acrylic,
children are the fruit of the body, the womb is a furnace.

Khakova Dam collapses. My dinner goes cold on the porcelain
plate and the last grain ship sets sail.

The man insists on generating a poem
in the style of [insert famous name], proving just how easy
it is to create. Machine poem reads: *God. Ablaze. Moon. Time.*

Who will eat this winter. The women's voices are on a loop.
Whose offspring will survive. Nine miles of tender

flesh put in the way of destruction. Thirty thousand
vaginas, sixty thousand hands, cervixes billowing

in the December rain. You can't weave a solution to crisis,
but there is always reproduction. When will an AI cry.

Here we sit. Here we stand. Soon the machine will
replace our organs — the body is a base facility.

For the length of a looping banner there's a poet shedding tears
on a lilac carpet. There's a poet. There's a processing.
The blood and bone of data. Deep saved in the body.

SATURNALIA

In the loudspeaker of a quarry I call
the lavish weather home. I slide
through the slick on my knees, burn
clocks, thumb the wax into being like
a god conjuring heartbeats. A womb, a torso,
a beetled pomegranate. Sweet medlar that rots
before it's ripe enough to eat. Before the match
is struck. A bottle is stuffed with a red rag flung
from a brook and I am the glass, shattering.
Because the butterfly. Because the oil is the I
that burns between ocean and crux. Wading in
the landslide of the house I've lost, the reckless
say there is nothing to do but leave. The only doubt
is duration. Because heartbreak. Another kind of mercy.

I HOLD THIS FRAGILE SPHERE

of earth
and sit up on the long barrow
to see myself a minuscule speck
on the sphere at the end of the day
at the end of the world and tell
myself there could be more time
and the waters of the Severn promise
me they've always been to sea
and the neolithic souls promise
they've forever crossed between worlds
and that evening the larks crowd in
with the brome grass and molluscs,
the bee orchids and oolite undoing all
the binaries and bringing the outside
inside out and for a few hours
I feel completely held by the intimacy
of our strangeness multiplying
in tender bonds on this tiny sphere
of earth.

Leaning in to the trouble. The lines 'broken hearted / in Van Diemen's land' are from a ballad about poachers deported to Van Diemen's Land (Tasmania). lutruwita is the indigenous Nuenonne / Palawa kani name for Tasmania.

No one wants to talk about the facts is, in part, a found poem. Sources include Culpeper's Herbal, Twitter, Stroud Textile Trust, Tuckers Hall, Plantlife, Museum in the Park, Rodborough Fields & Frome Banks Preservation Group, The National Trust.

Town has no history except it be that of the rise and peaceful progress of the woollen cloth trade. The title is a quote from Black's *Guide to Gloucestershire* (1878).

Hand Me Down is a cento. The sources are William Carlos Williams, Robert Browning, Edward Fitzgerald, Wilfred Owen.

Bodies remember such histories, even when we forget them. The title is a quote from Sara Ahmed in 'A Phenomenology of Whiteness' *Feminist Theory* 8:149 (2007) .

Self-Self considers Historical Self; or, why talk about these people when we can shy away. In *Citizen* (2014), Claudia Rankine talks about the friendship between the self selves of black and white women that turns to confrontation in the meeting of historical selves.

Letter from a sixteen-year-old white girl includes phrases from Letters and Memoranda of Eliza Lucas Pinckney 1740-1762.

Don't give me anything as mangled as this feeling. The title is inspired by a line in Megan Fernandes' poem 'Dignity,' 'I want everything as cheap and damaged as this feeling.'

Class War Pep Talk to Flock Wallpaper. 'Non-U' was a term coined by the linguist Alan S.C. Ross and used by author Nancy Mitford in her essay 'The English Aristocracy' (1956). The 'U' refers to upper class and 'non-U' to the aspiring middle classes.

Sentient includes original drawings by Susie Hetherington (Yew Tree Press, 2021).

What the Watercourse Carries. The grey italicised phrases are from attempted translations by Patrick Sims-Williams (2007) and Bernard Thomas Mees (2009) of the only fragment of Brittonic Celt in written form in existence, from a curse tablet at the Roman Baths, Bath.

Secrets of Matter and Spirit. The title is a quote from Carl Jung, 'The realm of the psyche is immeasurably great and filled with living reality. At its brink lies the secret of matter and of spirit.' *Letters* Vol. II, (1976).

We become with each other or not at all. The title is a quote from Donna Harraway *Staying with the Trouble: Making Kin in the Chthulucene* (2016).

Embrace The Base. 'Carry Greenham home, yes' and 'Here we sit, here we stand' are lyrics from the song 'Carry Greenham Home' by Peggy Seeger.

I wade the river searching for home has a rhythm that is inspired by Alice Oswald's poem, 'Dunt: a poem for a dried up river' — the Dunt is a tributary of the Churn, a river which runs throughout this book. Deae Matres is the Latin name given to the statue of the three mother goddesses explored in this poem. They are also called Sulevaie, associated with the name of an ancient Celtic goddess worshipped in Britain, Gaul and Galicia; some researchers have suggested the Sulevaie is a triune version of Sulis Minerva, the hybrid Romano-Celt goddess worshipped at Bath.

All images used are out of copyright. Teasel's illustration is of a fuller's teasel from F.A. Brockhaus *Brockhaus Konversations-Lexikon* (1908).

ACKNOWLEDGEMENTS

Some of the poems in this collection have been published, sometimes in slightly different form. Thanks to *The Poetry Review, The Sunday Telegraph, Places of Poetry,* BBC Upload, The Outposted Project, *Ink, Sweat and Tears, The Rialto, Magma, Raceme, Fenland Poetry Journal, 14, Finished Creatures, Allegro, Anthropocene, Bad Lilies,* Yew Tree Press, The Roman Baths at Bath, Fireside Books, Gloucestershire Wildlife Trust, International Dylan Thomas Day competition, Geoffrey Dearmer Prize, National Poetry Competition. I am so grateful to the curators of 'Invoking Absence' (Hallidays Mill, Chalford, Sep 2021), 'Plant Communitas' (Museum in the Park, Stroud, April 2022) and 'Between Earth and Sky' (Periscope Arts, September 2023) for showing my work.

Thank you, Pascale Petit, wise and tender mentor who encouraged me in the early stages of this collection's development; thank you also to the teachers who nudged me on my way as I brought the work together: Jay Bernard, Fiona Benson, Mimi Khalvati, Martha Sprackland, Helen Mort, Caroline Bird. Thank you to Arts Council England for the Developing Your Creative Practice Grant which made the research and writing of these poems possible. I am also very grateful for generous writing residencies at Stroudwater Textile Trust, Corinium Museum and the Monica Sjöö Curatorial Collective which gave me the focus and time to think and dream and write. Warm thanks to the whole Broken Sleep Team, especially Charley Barnes and Aaron Kent for their astute editorial guidance.

Deep gratitude to my fellow travellers for the camaraderie - the writing friends, musicians and artists who have collaborated and conversed, fedback on my poems and fired me up when the flames were guttering, especially Philip Rush, Alice Willitts, Emma Kernahan, Sasha Neale, Nathalie Edwards, Hannah Linfoot, Susie Hetherington, Vasiliki Albedo, Lucy Holme, Alun Hughes, Caleb Parkin, Patricia Brien, Su Fahy, Oonagh Davies, Joff Elphick, Claire Collison, Mara Simpson, the Dialect Writers community, Stuart Butler and the Radical Stroud Collective. To Ian Mackintosh for his unparalleled knowledge of local history. Everlasting love to the Brighton massive Claire Hines, Zoe Lawrence and Marni McArthur. To the unrivalled joy of the Saturday Swim Club fam who understand what it truly means to be still and listen: Kath Broomfield, Clare Burkey, Nina Cox, Lucy Harvey, Helen Haynes, Chantel Hodgson, Anna Kay, Soph Mumford, Kirstie Phipps, Lynsey Pollard.

Love, love, love and thanks to my family, especially to Mum for all the books through the years, to Jason and our shared affection for the Churn, to Marni and Bay for the everyday joy and to Mikey, who makes all of this possible.

LAY OUT YOUR UNREST

9 781916 938205